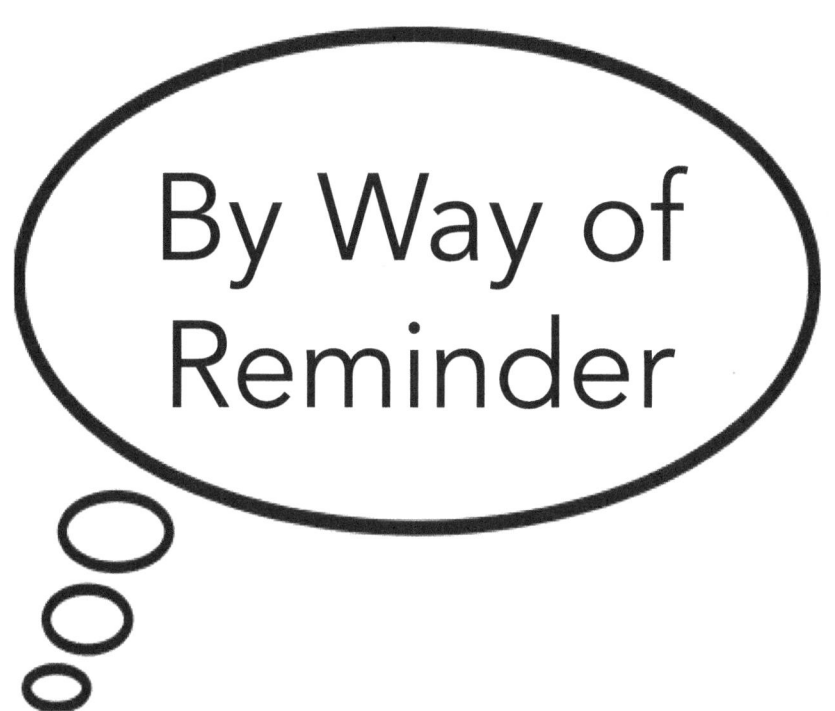

By Way of Reminder

Bible Lists
for Memorization & Reference

Cloyce Sutton II

© 2020 One Stone Press.
All rights reserved. No part of this book may be reproduced in any form without written permission of the publisher.

Published by:
One Stone Press
979 Lovers Lane
Bowling Green, KY 42103

Printed in the United States of America

All biblical references are based upon the
New American Standard Bible.

ISBN: 978-1-941422-55-7

www.onestone.com

Contents

Foreword 7

OLD TESTAMENT LISTS
Key OT Dates 10
Hebrew Alphabet 11
Books of the OT 12
Jewish Calendar 13
Jewish Festivals 14
Time Periods of OT History 15
Biblical Empires & Kingdoms 15
OT Weights & Measures 16-17
Days of Creation 18
Twelve Tribes of Israel 18
Plagues Against Egypt 19
Ten Commandments 20
Types of Sacrifices 20
Clean & Unclean Animals 21
Cities of Refuge 21
Levitical Cities 22
Layout of the Israelite Camp 23
Israelite Military Censuses 24
Levitical Censuses 25
Judges of Israel 26
Kings of Israel and Judah 27
Returns From Exile 28
Chronology of the Literary Prophets 29
OT Names for God 30

NEW TESTAMENT LISTS
Key NT Dates 32
Greek Alphabet 33
Books of the NT 34
Periods in the Life of Christ 34
New Testament Officials 35
Herods in the New Testament 36
Twelve Apostles 37

By Way of Reminder

Other Apostles 37
Jesus' Parables 38-39
Jesus' Miracles 40-41
Jesus' "I AM" Claims 41
Post-Resurrection Appearances of Jesus 42
Periods in the Life of Paul 42
Cities of Paul's First Journey 43
Cities of Paul's Second Journey 44
Cities of Paul's Third Journey 45
Cities of Paul's Journey to Rome 46
Seven Cities of Asia 46

SPECIAL LISTS
The Story of the Bible 48-49
Beatitudes 50
Model Prayer 50
Spiritual Gifts 51
Deeds of the Flesh 52
Fruit of the Spirit 52
Character of Love 53
Armor of God 53
Qualifications of Elders 54-55
Qualifications of Deacons 56
Christian Graces 57

BIBLE TOPICS & MEMORY VERSES
The Bible 60
God 60
Jesus Christ 60
The Holy Spirit 60
Man 60
Sin 60-61
Faith 61
Repentance 61
Baptism 61
Salvation 61
Forgiveness 61
The Church 61-62
Growth 62
Anger 62

Contents

Assurance 62
Children 62
Comfort 62
Doubt 62
Death 62
Depression 62
Discouragement 62
Encouragement 63
Envy 63
Family 63
Fathers 63
Fear 63
Friendship 63-64
Gossip 64
Gratitude 64
Grief 64
Guilt 64
Happiness 64
Health 64
Homosexuality 64
Hope 64
Humility 65
Husbands 65
Joy 65
Laziness 65
Loneliness 65
Love for God 65
Love for Others 65-66
Lust 66
Lying 66
Marriage 66
Men 66
Money 66
Mothers 66
Obedience 66
Parents 66
Patience 67
Peace 67
Persecution 67
Perseverance 67

Pornography	67
Praise	67
Prayer	67
Pride	68
Sex & Lust	68
Sickness	68
Temptation	68
Thankfulness	68
Wealth	68
Wives	68
Women	68
Work	68
Worry	68
Worship	69
Youth	69
Zeal	69

Foreword

"Therefore, I will always be ready to remind you of these things, even though you already know them, and have been established in the truth which is present with you. I consider it right, as long as I am in this earthly dwelling, to stir you up by way of reminder, knowing that the laying aside of my earthly dwelling is imminent, as also our Lord Jesus Christ has made clear to me. And I will also be diligent that at any time after my departure you will be able to call these things to mind," (2 Peter 1.12-15).

In these verses, the apostle Peter stated his purpose for writing: to remind his readers of things they already knew, so that they could recall them as needed. It's not surprising, then, Peter speaks of "knowledge" eight times in this brief letter (2 Peter 1.2, 3, 5, 6, 8; 2.12, 20; 3.18). He ends the letter with an exhortation to "grow in the grace and knowledge of our Lord and Savior Jesus Christ" (3.18).

The purpose of knowledge for Christians is to strengthen us against temptation and to build character (2 Peter 1.2-11). That's why we must spend time in Bible study and why we must be able to recall what we've studied.

This book is a listing of information that can help you in your Bible studies. It's a what-to-know book, not a how-to-do-it book. It contains various lists related to or taken from the Bible. Much of this you may have learned long ago in church or family Bible classes or studies. If that's the case, this may serve as a refresher course. If you never learned the information, or you've forgotten it, this may serve as a springboard for further learning.

The first half of this booklet contains lists of the most important things, people, places, and events in the Bible. These can help you mentally organize the vast amount of information in the Bible. Some of the lists are elementary and simple. Some are more advanced and complicated. Start with the easy lists and add the more challenging ones as you go.

By Way of Reminder

The second half of the booklet includes a number of suggested Bible verses to memorize. The best way to fight temptation and sin is to memorize Scripture (Psalm 119.11). First, memorize verses that will help you personally in your spiritual life. Second, memorize verses that you can share with others. Finally, memorize verses on a broader range of Bible topics.

Also, remember the dates presented here are only educated guesses.

I also want to thank those who helped proofread this edition: Robin Franks, Sara Smalley, Jodi Stanford, and Ron Lanning.

I especially want to thank my wife Alethea. Her devotion, encouragement, and example have been constant in more than thirty years of marriage. It is with my deepest affection and love that I dedicate this volumen to her.

May God bless your efforts.

Cloyce Sutton II

Old Testament Lists

By Way of Reminder
Key OT Dates
All dates are "BC"

Date (B.C.)	Event
2166-1991	Abraham
1446	The Exodus
1406	Entrance into Canaan
1385-1050	Judges Period
1050-1010	Saul Reigns
1010-970	David Reigns
970-930	Solomon Reigns
930	Kingdom Splits Between Judah & Israel
721	Israel & Samaria Fall to Assyria
612	Fall of Nineveh to Babylon
609	Fall of Haran & Death of Josiah
605	Fall of Carchemish, First Jerusalem Siege
597	Second Jerusalem Siege
586	Third Jerusalem Siege & Fall
539	Fall of Babylon to Persians
538	First Return under Zerubbabel
536-516	Temple Rebuilt
458	Second Return under Ezra
444	Third Return under Nehemiah
433	Malachi's Prophecy & End of the Old Testament

Hebrew Alphabet
See the headings in Psalm 119

Letter	Name	Sound	English
א	Alef	silent	
ב	Bet	b	b
ג	Gimel	g	g
ד	Dalet	d	d
ה	He	h	h
ו	Vav	v	v
ז	Zayin	z	z
ח	Chet	ch as in Bach	ch
ט	Tet	t	t
י	Yod	y	y
כ	Kaf	k	k
ל	Lamed	l	l
מ	Mem	m	m
נ	Nun	n	n
ס	Samek	s	s
ע	Ayin	silent	
פ	Pe	p or f	p
צ	Tsade	ts	ts
ק	Qof	q	q
ר	Resh	r	r
ש	Sin	s or sh	s or sh
ת	Tav		t

By Way of Reminder
Books of the Old Testament

<u>English Arrangement</u>

BOOKS OF LAW
    Genesis, Exodus, Leviticus, Numbers, Deuteronomy

BOOKS OF HISTORY
    Joshua, Judges, Ruth, 1-2 Samuel, 1-2 Kings,
    1-2 Chronicles, Ezra, Nehemiah, Esther

BOOKS OF POETRY
    Job, Psalms, Proverbs, Ecclesiastes, Song of Solomon

BOOKS OF PROPHECY
    Major Prophets
    Isaiah, Jeremiah, Lamentations, Ezekiel, Daniel
    Minor Prophets
    Hosea, Joel, Amos, Obadiah, Jonah, Micah, Nahum,
    Habakkuk, Zephaniah, Haggai, Zechariah, Malachi

<u>Hebrew Arrangement</u>

TORAH
    Genesis, Exodus, Leviticus, Numbers, Deuteronomy

FORMER PROPHETS
    Joshua, Judges, 1-2 Samuel, 1-2 Kings

LATTER PROPHETS
    Isaiah, Jeremiah, Ezekiel, Hosea, Joel, Amos, Obadiah,
    Jonah, Micah, Nahum, Habakkuk, Zephaniah, Haggai,
    Zechariah, Malachi

THE WRITINGS
    Psalms, Job, Proverbs, Ruth, Song of Solomon,
    Ecclesiastes, Lamentations, Esther, Daniel, Ezra,
    Nehemiah, 1 & 2 Chronicles

Jewish Calendar

Month	Ours	Farming
1 - Nisan	March/April	Barley harvest
2 - Iyyar	April/May	General harvest
3 - Silvan	May/June	Wheat Harvest, Vine tending
4 - Tammuz	June/July	First grapes
5 - Ab	July/August	Grapes, figs, olives
6 - Elus	August/September	Vintage
7 - Tishri	September/October	Plowing
8 - Marchesvan	October/November	Grain planting
9 - Kislev	November/December	
10 - Tebet	December/January	Spring growth
11 - Shebat	January/February	Winter figs
12 - Adar	February/March	Pulling flax, almonds bloom
Adar Sheni	Intercalary month	

By Way of Reminder

Jewish Festivals

Day	Date	Reference	Purpose
Passover (Pesach)	14 Nisan	Exodus 12; Leviticus 23:4-8	Deliverance from Egypt
Pentecost (Shavuoth)	6 Sivan	Deuteronomy 16:9-12; Leviticus 23:15-21	Harvest
9th of Ab (Tish'ah be'ab)	9 Ab		Destruction of temple (586 BC)
Day of Atonement (Yom Kippur)	10 Tishri	Leviticus 16; 23:26-32	Sins of the nation
Feast of Tabernacles (Succoth)	15 - 21 Tishri	Nehemiah 8; Leviticus 23:33-36	Wilderness wanderings
Dedication (Chanukah)	25 Kislev	John 10:22	Restoration of the temple (164 BC)
Lots (Purim)	13 - 14 Adar	Esther 9	Jews spared from Haman

Time Periods of Old Testament History

1. Primeval .... (from the creation)
2. Patriarchal .... (from the call of Abraham)
3. Bondage ....(from the descent into Egypt)
4. Wanderings ....(from the exodus from Egypt)
5. Conquests ....(from the crossing of the Jordan River)
6. Judges ....(from the death of Joshua)
7. United Kingdom ....(from King Saul)
8. Divided Kingdom .... (from the death of Solomon)
9. Judah Alone .... (from the fall of Samaria)
10. Exile .... (from the fall of Jerusalem)
11. Restoration ....(from the first return)
12. Intertestamental.......... (from the close of the Old Testament)

Biblical Empires and Kingdoms
All dates are BC

1. Egyptian Kingdoms .... (3000-332)
2. Akkadian Kingdoms .... (2334-2154)
3. Hittite Empire .... (1600-1178)
4. Assyrian Empire .... (1300-610)
5. Philistines .... (1200-586)
6. Syrian Kingdom .... (940-732)
7. Babylonian Kingdom .... (625-539)
8. Persians .... (539-331)
9. Greeks .... (336-323)
10. Ptolemaic (Egyptian) Kingdom .... (323-30)
11. Seleucid (Syrian) Empire .... (312-63)
12. Maccabean Dynasty .... (137-37)
13. Roman Empire ...... (30 BC to the end of the New Testament)

By Way of Reminder

Old Testament Weights and Measures

Type	Measure	Reference	English
Weight	Gerah	Exodus 30:13	0.022 oz
	Beka = 10 gerahas	Exodus 38:26	0.22 oz
	Shekel = 2 bekas	Exodus 30:13	0.4 oz
	Mina = 50 shekels	1 Kings 10:17	1.1 lbs
	Talent = 60 minas	Exodus 38:24-25	66 lbs
Liquid	Log	Leviticus 14:10	0.67 pts
	Kab = 4 logs	Liquid Kab not in the Old Testament	2.62 pts
	Hin = 2 kabs	Exodus 29:40	1 gal
	Bath = 6 hins	1 Kings 7:23-26	6 gal
	Homer = 10 baths	Ezekiel 45:13-14	60 gal

Old Testament Weights and Measures

Type	Measure	Reference	English
Dry	Log	Not in the Old Testament	0.32 qts
	Kab = 4 logs	2 Kings 6:25	1.3 qts
	Omer = 7 logs	Exodus 16:16, 36	2.3 qts
	Seah (measure) = 6 kabs	Genesis 18:6; 2 Kings 7:1	1 pk or 11 qts
	Ephah = 3 seahs	Exodus 16:36; 29:40	0.75 bu
	Lethech = 5 ephahs	Hosea 3:2	3 bu and 3 pks
	Homer = 2 lethechs	Leviticus 27:16; Numbers 11:32	7.5 bu
Length	Digit (finger)	Jeremiah 52:21	3/4 in
	Handbreadth	Exodus 25:25	3 in
	Span = Outstretched hand	Exodus 28:16	9 in
	Cubit = elbow to fingertip	Genesis 6:15	18 in
	Reed	Ezekiel 42:16-18	6 cubits
	Gomed	Judges 3:16	2/3 cubit

By Way of Reminder
Days of Creation
See Genesis 1

Day 1 .... Heavens, earth, light, dark
Day 2 .... Expanse in the heavens
Day 3 .... Land, seas, vegetation
Day 4 .... Sun, moon, stars
Day 5 .... Sea creatures, birds
Day 6 .... Land animals, man
Day 7 .... God rested

Twelve Tribes of Israel
See Genesis 29:31-30:24; 35:16-21
By mother, in birth order (meaning of name)

<u>By Leah</u>
1. Reuben (Behold, a son)
2. Simeon (Hearing)
3. Levi (Attachment)
4. Judah (Praise)

<u>By Bilhah (Rachel's Handmaid)</u>
5. Dan (Judgment)
6. Naphtali (Wrestle)

<u>By Zilpah (Leah's Handmaid)</u>
7. Gad (Good fortune)
8. Asher (Happy)

<u>By Leah</u>
9. Issachar (Reward)
10. Zebulun (Abode)

<u>By Rachel</u>
11. Joseph (May he add)
12. Benjamin (Son of the right hand)

Plagues Against Egypt
See Exodus 7-12, especially Exodus 12:12

Plague	Reference	Egyptian Deity Targeted
Water to blood	Exodus 7:14-25	Khnum - guardian of the Nile Hapi - spirit of the Nile Osiris - Nile was bloodstream Neith - protector of the fish in the Nile
Frogs	Exodus 8:1-15	Heqt - form of a frog
Gnats / Lice	Exodus 8:16-19	
Flies	Exodus 8:20-32	Uachit - represented by flies
Death of cattle	Exodus 9:1-7	Hathor - form of a cow Apis - bull god Mnevis - sacred bull
Boils	Exodus 9:8-12	Imhotep - god of medicine Sekhmet - controlled epidemics
Hail	Exodus 9:13-35	Nut - sky goddess Isis - goddess of life Seth - protector of crops
Locusts	Exodus 10:1-20	Isis - goddess of life Seth - protector of crops
Darkness	Exodus 10:21-29	Re, Aten, Atum, Horus - all sun gods
Death of firstborn	Exodus 11:1-12:36	Osiris - giver of life Pharaoh - as deity

By Way of Reminder

Ten Commandments
See Exodus 20

1. You shall have no other gods before me.
2. You shall not make any idols.
3. You shall not take the Lord's name in vain.
4. You shall remember the Sabbath.
5. You shall honor your father & mother.
6. You shall not murder.
7. You shall not commit adultery.
8. You shall not steal.
9. You shall not bear false witness.
10. You shall not covet.

Types of Sacrifices
See Leviticus 1 - 6

Type	Reference	Purpose
Burnt Offering	Leviticus 1	Atonement, Dedication
Grain Offering	Leviticus 2	Thankfulness, First fruits
Peace Offering	Leviticus 3	Fellowship, Freewill offerings, Vows
Sin Offering	Leviticus 4	Unintentional sin (individual or national)
Guilt Offering	Leviticus 5 - 6	Uncleanness, Civil law violations

Clean and Unclean Animals
See Leviticus 11 and Deuteronomy 14

Type	Text	Clean	Unclean
Mammals	Leviticus 11:3-7; Deuteronomy 14:6-8	Cloven hooves; chew cud	Any other mammals
Birds	Leviticus 11:13-19; Deuteronomy 14:11-20	Those not specifically forbidden	Birds of prey or Scavengers
Reptiles	Leviticus 11:29-30	None	All
Water Animals	Leviticus 11:9-12; Deuteronomy 14:9-10	Must have fins and scales	Any other fish
Insects	Leviticus 11:20-23	Grasshopper family	Any winged quadrupeds

Cities of Refuge
See Numbers 35:9-15; Joshua 20

West of the Jordan River (Tribal Territory)
1. Hebron (Judah)
2. Shechem (Ephraim)
3. Kedesh (Naphtali)

East of the Jordan River (Tribal Territory)
1. Golan (Manasseh)
2. Ramoth-Gilead (Gad)
3. Bezer (Reuben)

By Way of Reminder

Levitical Cities
See Numbers 35:1-8; Joshua 21; 1 Chronicles 6:54-81
(A = Aaronite city; G = Gershonite; M = Merarite; K = Kohathite)

Tribe	City (Levitical Clan)
Judah and Simeon	Kiriaht Arba or Hebron (A), Libnah (A), Jattir (A), Eshtemoa (A), Holon (A), Debir (A), Ain (A), Juttah (A), Beth Shemesh (A)
Benjamin	Gibeon (A), Geba (A), Anathoth (A), Almon (A)
Ephraim	Shechem (K), Gezer (K), Kibzaim (K), Beth Horon (K)
Dan	Elteke (K), Gibbethon (K), Aijalon (K), Gath-Rimmon (K)
Manasseh	Taanach (K), Gath-Rimmon (K), Golan (G), Be-eshterah (G)
Issachar	Kishion (G), Daberath (G), Jarmuth (G), En-gannim (G)
Asher	Mishal (G), Abdon (G), Helkath (G), Rehob (G)
Naphtali	Kedesh in Galilee (G), Hammoth-dor (G), Kartan (G)
Zebulun	Jokneam (M), Kartah (M), Dimnah (M), Nahalal (M)
Reuben	Bezer (M), Jahaz (M), Kedemoth (M), Mephaath (M)
Gad	Ramoth in Gilead (M), Mahanaim (M), Heshbon (M), Jazer (M)
Simeon	Included with the cities of Judah

Bible Lists

Israel's Camp in the Wilderness
See Numbers 1-2, 10

#15 - Naphtali (Ahira - 53,400)	#14 - Asher (Pagiel - 41,500)	#13 - Dan (Ahiezer - 62,700)
#12 - Benjamin (Abidan - 35,400)	#5 - Merari (6,200)	#1 - Judah (Nahshon - 74,600)
#11 - Manasseh (Gamaliel - 32,200)	#4 - Gershon (7,500) / Tabernacle / Moses, Aaron and Priests	#2 - Issachar (Nethanel - 54,400)
#10 - Ephraim (Elishama - 40,500)	#9 - Kohath (8,600)	#3 - Zebulun (Eliab - 57,400)
#8 - Gad (Eliasaph - 45,650)	#7 - Simeon (Shelumiel - 59,300)	#6 - Reuben (Elizur - 46,500)

Marching order; tribe or clan name; tribal head; number of adult males

By Way of Reminder

Israelite Military Censuses
See Numbers 1 and 26

Tribe	1st Generation (Numbers 1)	2nd Generation (Numbers 26)	Change
Reuben	46,500	43,730	-2,770
Simeon	59,300	22,200	-37,100
Gad	45,650	40,500	-5,150
Judah	74,600	76,500	1,900
Issachar	54,400	64,300	9,900
Zebulun	57,400	60,500	3,100
Ephraim	40,500	32,500	-8,000
Manasseh	32,200	52,700	20,500
Benjamin	35,400	45,600	10,200
Dan	62,700	64,400	1,700
Asher	41,500	53,400	11,900
Naphtali	53,400	45,400	-8,000
Totals	603,550	601,730	-1,820

Levitical Censuses
See Numbers 3-4; 26:57-62

Clan	Numbers 4:34-35	Numbers 3:21-39	Numbers 26:57-62
Gershon	2,630	7,500	-
Kohath	2,750	8,600	-
Merari	3,200	6,200	-
Totals	8,580	22,000	23,000

By Way of Reminder

Judges of Israel

Judge	Tribe	Enemy
Othniel	Judah	Mesopotamians
Ehud	Benjamin	Moabites
Shamgar	?	Philistines
Deborah	Ephraim	Canaanites
Gideon	Manasseh	Midianites
Tola	Issachar	?
Jair	?	?
Jephthah	?	Ammonites
Ibzan	Judah	?
Elon	Zebulun	?
Abdon	Ephraim	?
Samson	Dan	Philistines
Eli	Levi	Philistines
Samuel	Levi	Philistines

Kings of Israel and Judah

Dates for Israelite kings are based upon Edwin R. Thiele's work. Overlapping dates indicate coregencies. All dates are "BC."

THE UNITED KINGDOM
All twelve tribes under one ruler

1. Saul (1050-1010)
2. David (1010-970)
3. Solomon (970-930)

THE DIVIDED KINGDOM

KINGS OF JUDAH
The southern kingdom, based in Jerusalem.

1. Rehoboam (930-913)
2. Abijam (913-910)
3. Asa (910-870)
4. Jehoshaphat (873-848)
5. Jehoram (854-841)
6. Ahaziah (841)
7. Athaliah (841-835)
8. Joash (835-796)
9. Amaziah (796-767)
10. Azariah (791-739)
11. Jotham (750-732)
12. Ahaz (732-715)
13. Hezekiah (715-687)
14. Manasseh (697-643)
15. Amon (643-641)
16. Josiah (641-609)
17. Jehoahaz (609)
18. Jehoiakim (609-598)
19. Jehoiachin (598-597)
20. Zedekiah (597-586)

KINGS OF ISRAEL
The northern kingdom, based mainly in Samaria.

1. Jeroboam (931-910)
2. Nadab (910-909)
3. Baasha (909-886)
4. Elah (886-885)
5. Zimri (885)
6. Tibni (885? A rival to Omri)
7. Omri (885-874)
8. Ahab (874-853)
9. Ahaziah (853-852)
10. Joram (852-841)
11. Jehu (841-814)
12. Jehoahaz (814-798)
13. Joash (798-782)
14. Jeroboam II (793-753)
15. Zechariah (753-752)
16. Shallum (752)
17. Menahem (752-742)
18. Pekahiah (742-740)
19. Pekah (752-732)
20. Hoshea (732-722)

By Way of Reminder

Returns from Exile
All dates are "BC."

Return	First	Second	Third
Text	Ezra 1 - 6	Ezra 7 - 10	Nehemiah 1 - 13
Date	538	458	444
Leaders	Sheshbazzar Zerubbabel Jeshua	Ezra	Nehemiah
Persian King	Cyrus	Artaxerxes Longimanus	Artaxerxes Longimaus
Number Returning	49,697 total	1775 total	?
Events	Rebuilding temple begins; sacrifices resume, Feast of Tabernacles; temple finished (516)	Problems with intermarriage	Wall rebuilt in 52 days; wall dedicated; Law is read.

Chronology of the Literary Prophets

All dates are "BC." Nations at top are the primary audience.

Israel	Judah	Foreign Nations
Assyrian Period		
Amos (760)	Isaiah (740-700)	Jonah (770)
Babylonian Period		
	Habakkuk (630) Zephaniah (627) Jeremiah (627-580) Daniel (605-530) Ezekiel (592-570)	Nahum (650)
Persian Period		
	Haggai (520) Zechariah (520-518) Joel (500) Malachi (433)	Obadiah (500)

By Way of Reminder

Old Testament Names for God

Hebrew	English	Text	Significance
Elohim	God	Genesis 1:1	Power and might
Adonai	Lord or God	Psalm 2:4	Lord; one with authority
YHWH	LORD	Deuteronomy 7:9	Covenant name of God; unpronounced by Jews
El-Elyon	God Most High	Genesis 14:17-24	God Who is above all things
El-Ro'i	God Who Sees	Genesis 16:13	God's omniscience and omnipresence
El-Shaddai	God Almighty	Genesis 17:1	God's omnipotence
El-'Olam	God Everlasting	Genesis 21:33 Isaiah 40:28	God's eternal nature
YHWH-Yir'eh	LORD will provide	Genesis 22:14	God's providential care
YHWH-Nissi	LORD is my banner	Exodus 17:15	God leads to victory
YHWH-Tzeva'ot	LORD of Hosts	1 Samuel 1:3	God's innumerable heavenly army
YHWH-Shalom	LORD is peace	Judges 6:24	God brings peace
YHWH-'Asah	LORD our Maker	Psalm 95:6	God as Creator
YHWH-Tzedeknu	LORD our righteousnes	Jeremiah 23:6	God's righteousness which He bestows
YHWH-Shammah	LORD is there	Ezekiel 48:35	God's presence

New Testament Lists

By Way of Reminder

Key New Testament Dates

Date	Event
6 BC	Jesus born
4 BC	Herod the Great dies
AD 7	Jesus appears in the temple at age 12
AD 26 (early)	John the Baptizer begins his ministry
AD 26 (late)	Jesus is baptized
AD 30 (spring)	Jesus is crucified
AD 30 (summer)	Day of Pentecost; Spirit poured out
AD 32	Conversion of Saul of Tarsus
AD 35	Paul's first Jerusalem visit
AD 44	Church persecuted by Herod Agrippa I
AD 45	Epistle of James written
AD 46-47	Paul's first journey
AD 48 / 49	Jerusalem council
AD 49-52	Paul's second journey
AD 53-56	Paul's third journey
AD 57	Paul arrested in Jerusalem
AD 60-62	1st Roman imprisonment
AD 64	Deaths of Paul and Peter
AD 70	Destruction of Jerusalem
AD 90	John's writings
AD 98	John dies

Greek Alphabet

Letter	Name	Sound	English
α, Α	Alpha	a as in father	a
β, Β	Beta	b	b
γ, Γ	Gamma	g	g
δ, Δ	Delta	d	d
ε, Ε	Epsilon	e as in met	e
ζ, Ζ	Zeta	z	z
η, Η	Eta	e as in obey	ē
θ, Θ	Theta	th	th
ι, Ι	Iota	i as in thing	i
κ, Κ	Kappa	k	k
λ, Λ	Lambda	l	l
μ, Μ	Mu	m	m
ν, Ν	Nu	n	n
ξ, Ξ	Xi	x as in axis	x
ο, Ο	Omicron	o as in not	o
π, Π	Pi	p	p
ρ, Ρ	Rho	r	r
σ, Σ	Sigma	s	s
τ, Τ	Tau	t	t
υ, Υ	Upsilon	u as in push	u or y
φ, Φ	Phi	ph	ph
χ, Χ	Chi	ch as in loch	ch
ψ, Ψ	Psi	ps as in lips	ps
ω, Ω	Omega	o as in tone	ō

By Way of Reminder
Books of the New Testament

Biography
    Matthew, Mark, Luke, John

History
    Acts

Epistles
    Paul's Letters
    Romans, 1 and 2 Corinthians, Galatians, Ephesians, Philippians, Colossians, 1 and 2 Thessalonians, 1 and 2 Timothy, Titus, Philemon

    General Letters
    Hebrews, James, 1 and 2 Peter, 1, 2, and 3 John, Jude

Prophecy (Apocalyptic)
    Revelation

Periods in the Life of Christ

1. Preparation .... (birth - John the Baptist's ministry)
2. Obscurity .... (baptism - cleansing the temple)
3. Popularity .... (Nazareth sermon - feeding the 5,000)
4. Withdrawal .... (Peter's confession - Zacchaeus)
5. Passion .... (triumphal entry - crucifixion)
6. Victory .... (resurrection - ascension)

New Testament Officials

Ruler	Position	Reference
Augustus	Caesar	Luke 2:1
Tiberius	Caesar	Luke 3:1
Claudius	Caesar	Acts 11:27; 18:1
Pontius Pilate	Procurator	Luke 3:1; 23:1
M. Antonius Felix	Procurator	Acts 23 - 24
Porcius Festus	Procurator	Acts 24:27
Quirinius	Governor	Luke 2:2
Lysanias	Tetrarch	Luke 3:1
Cornelius	Centurion	Acts 10:1
Sergius Paulus	Proconsul	Acts 13:7
Gallio	Proconsul	Acts 18:12
Claudius Lysias	Commander	Acts 23:26; 21:31
Julius	Centurion	Acts 27:1
Publius	Leading man	Acts 28:7
Erastus	Treasurer	Romans 16:23
Aretas	King	2 Corinthians 11:32

By Way of Reminder

Herods in the New Testament
Boldface names are how they are known.

Name	Reference	Information
Herod (the Great)	Matthew 2:1-9; Luke 1:5	King at Jesus' birth
(Herod) **Archelaus**	Matthew 2:22	Succeeded father; king when Jesus was in Egypt
Herod (Antipas)	Matthew 14:1-12; Mark 6:14-29; Luke 3:1; 13:31-35; 23:7-12	Married Herodias; executed John the Baptizer; tried Jesus
(Herod) **Philip** (1)	Luke 3:1	Married Salome
(Herod) **Philip** (2)	Matthew 14:3; Mark 6:17	First husband of Herodias
Herodias	Matthew 14:1-12; Mark 6:14-29	Married to Philip (2), then to Antipas; mother of Salome
Salome	Matthew 14:1-12; Mark 6:14-29	Daughter of Herodias; wife of Philip (1)
Herod (Agrippa I)	Acts 12:1-24	Killed James the apostle
Herod **Agrippa** (II)	Acts 25:13-26:32	Tried Paul with Festus; son of Agrippa
Bernice	Acts 25:13	Sister and wife of Agrippa II; daughter of Agrippa I
Drusilla	Acts 24:24	Daughter of Agrippa I; wife of Felix

The Twelve Apostles

See Matthew 10:1-4; Mark 3:13-19; Luke 6:13-16; Acts 1:13

1. Simon Peter
2. Andrew
3. James (son of Zebedee)
4. John (son of Zebedee)
5. Philip
6. Bartholomew (Nathanael)
7. Thomas
8. Matthew
9. James the Less (son of Alphaeus)
10. Thaddeus (Judas, son of James)
11. Simon the Zealot
12. Judas Iscariot

Other "Apostles"

- Matthias (Acts 1:26)
- Barnabas (Acts 14:14)
- Paul (Acts 14:14; Romans 1:1; etc.)
- James, the Lord's brother (Galatians 1:19)
- Andronicus (Romans 16:7)
- Junias (Romans 16:7)
- Jesus (Hebrews 3:1)

Jesus' Parables

Parable	MT	MK	LK
Wedding Guests	9:14f	2:18ff	5:33ff
Patches on old garments	9:16	2:21	5:36
Wine & wineskins	9:17	2:22	5:37f
Sower	13:3-23	4:2-20	8:4-15
Mustard Seed	13:31f	4:30ff	13:18f
Fig Tree	21:19ff; 24:32f	13:28f	21:29ff
Landowner and tenants	21:33-41	12:1-12	20:9-19
Wise & foolish builders	7:24-27		6:47ff
Children in marketplace	11:16f		7:31f
Leaven	13:33		13:20f
Lost sheep	18:12ff		15:3-7
Wise steward	24:45-51		12:42-48
Tares	13:24-30		
Hidden Treasure	13:44		
Precious Pearl	13:45f		
Dragnet	13:47-50		
Householder	13:51ff		
Unmerciful servant	18:23-35		
Laborers in the vineyard	20:1-16		
Two sons	21:28-32		
Marriage of the king's son	22:1-14		
Ten virgins	25:1-13		

Jesus' Parables (cont.)

Parable	MT	MK	LK
Talents	25:14-30		
Sheep & goats	25:31-36		
Seed growing secrecly		4:26-29	
Door keeper		13:34-37	
Two debtors			7:36-50
Good Samaritan			10:25-37
Friend at midnight			11:5-10
Rich fool			12:16-21
Watchful servants			12:35-38
Barren fig tree			13:6-9
Chief seats			14:7-11
Feasts for the poor			14:12ff
Great supper			14:16-24
Tower			14:28ff
King			14:31-33
Lost coin			15:8-10
Lost son			15:11-32
Dishonest steward			16:1-9
Rich man & Lazarus			16:19-31
Master & servants			17:7-10
Persistent widow			18:1-8
Pharisees & tax collector			18:9-14
Minas			19:11-27

By Way of Reminder

Jesus' Miracles

Miracles	MT	MK	LK	JN
Water to wine				2:1-11
Feeding 5,000	14:15-21	6:35-44	9:12-17	6:5-15
Stilling the storm	8:23-27	4:35-41	8:22-25	
Walking on water	14:22-33	6:45-52		6:16-21
Tax money	17:24-27			
Feeding 4,000	15:32-39	8:1-9		
Withered fig tree	21:17-22	11:12-25		
1st catch of fish			5:1-11	
2nd catch of fish				21:1-14
Nobleman's son (Cana)				4:46-54
Blind man (Bethsaida)		8:22-26		
Man born blind				9:1-41
Raising Lazarus				11:1-45
Demon-possessed man	8:28-34	5:1-20	8:26-39	
Jairus' daughter	9:18-26	5:22ff, 35-43	8:41ff, 49-56	
Invalid at Bethesda				5:1-18
Woman with hemorrhage	9:20ff	5:25-34	8:43-48	
Paralytic at Capernaum	9:1-8	2:1-12	5:17-26	
Leper near Gennesaret	8:1-4	1:40-45	5:12-15	
Peter's mother-in-law	8:14-17	1:29-31	4:38-39	
Withered hand	12:9-14	3:1-6	6:6-11	
Child with demon	17:14-20	9:14-29	9:37-43	

Jesus' Miracles (cont.)

Miracles	MT	MK	LK	JN
Blind & mute demoniac	12:22		11:14	
Two blind men	9:27-31			
Mute demoniac	9:32-34			
Deaf-mute		7:31-37		
Sight to Bartimaeus	20:29-34	10:46-52	18:35-43	
Syrophoenician girl	15:21-28	7:24-30		
Centurion's servant	8:5-13		7:1-10	
Demoniac in synagogue		1:23-27	4:33-36	
Widow's son at Nain			7:11-16	
Woman cripple			13:10-17	
Man with dropsy			14:1-6	
Ten lepers			17:11-19	
Malchus' ear			22:49-51	18:10-11

Jesus' "I AM" Claims

1. "I am the *bread of life*" (John 6.35, 48, 51)
2. "I am the *light of the world*" (John 8.12; 9.5)
3. "I am the *door of the sheep*" (John 10.7, 9)
4. "I am the *good shepherd*" (John 10.11, 14)
5. "I am the *resurrection, and the life*" (John 11.25)
6. "I am the *way, the truth, and the life*" (John 14.6)
7. "I am the *true vine*" (John 15.1, 5)

By Way of Reminder

Post-Resurrection Appearances of Jesus
See Matthew 28; Mark 16; Luke 24; John 20-21; 1 Corinthians 15

1. To the women: Mary the mother of the sons of Zebedee, Salome, Joanna
2. To Mary Magdalene
3. To Simon Peter
4. To Cleopas & another disciple
5. To the apostles (without Thomas)
6. To the apostles (with Thomas)
7. To seven disciples (at the Sea of Tiberius)
8. To the disciples at a mountain in Galilee
9. To over 500 disciples
10. To James, the Lord's brother
11. To the disciples at his ascension
12. To Saul of Tarsus

Periods in the Life of Paul

1. Upbringing & opposition to Christianity
2. Conversion & early preaching
3. First preaching journey
4. Jerusalem meeting
5. Second preaching journey
6. Third preaching journey
7. Arrest & imprisonment
8. First Roman imprisonment
9. Second Roman imprisonment & death

Cities of Paul's First Journey

See Acts 13-14
Regions & provinces are italicized; cities implied by the routes taken (*)

OUTBOUND
- Antioch *(Syria)*
- Seleucia
- Salamis *(Cyprus)*
- Paphos *(Cyprus)*
- Perga *(Pamphylia)*
- Antioch *(Pisidia)*
- Iconium
- Lystra
- Derbe

RETURN
- Derbe *(Lycaonia)*
- Lystra *(Lycaonia)*
- Iconium
- Antioch *(Pisidia)*
- Perga *(Pamphylia)*
- Attalia *(Pamphylia)*
- Seleucia*
- Antioch *(Syria)*

By Way of Reminder
Cities of Paul's Second Journey
See Acts 15:36 - 18:22
Regions & provinces are italicized; cities implied by the routes taken (*)

OUTBOUND
- Antioch *(Syria)*
- *Cilicia*
- Derbe
- Lystra
- Iconium
- Antioch *(Pisidia)*
- *Phrygia*
- *Galatia*
- Troas
- Samothrace
- Neapolis
- Philippi
- Amphipolis
- Apollonia
- Thessalonica
- Berea
- Athens
- Corinth

RETURN
- Corinth
- Cenchrea
- Ephesus
- Caesarea Maritima
- Jerusalem*
- Antioch *(Syria)*

Cities of Paul's Third Journey
See Acts 18:23 - 21:26
Regions & provinces are italicized; cities implied by the routes taken (*)

OUTBOUND
- Antioch *(Syria)*
- Cilician Gates *(Galatia)*
- Derbe *(Galatia)*
- Lystra *(Galatia)*
- Iconium *(Galatia)*
- Antioch *(Pisidia)*
- *Phrygia*
- Ephesus

RETURN
- Troas*
- *Macedonia*
- *Greece*
- Philippi
- Troas
- Assos
- Mitylene
- Chios
- Samos
- Miletus
- Cos
- Rhodes
- Patara
- Tyre
- Ptolemais
- Caesarea Maritima
- Jerusalem

By Way of Reminder
Cities of Paul's Journey to Rome
See Acts 21:27 - 28:31
Regions & provinces are italicized

- Jerusalem
- Caesarea Maritima
- Sidon
- Cyprus
- *Cilicia*
- *Pamphylia*
- Myra *(Lycia)*
- Cnidus
- Salmone *(Crete)*
- Lasea *(Crete)*
- Fair Havens *(Crete)*
- Phoenix *(Crete)*
- Clauda
- Malta
- Syracuse
- Rhegium
- Puteoli
- Market of Appius
- Three Inns
- Rome

Seven Churches of Asia
Revelation 1:11; Chapters 2 - 3

1. Ephesus
2. Smyrna
3. Pergamum
4. Thyatira
5. Sardis
6. Philadelphia
7. Laodicea

Special Lists

By Way of Reminder
The Story of the Bible
In 20 Verses

OLD TESTAMENT (PROMISE)
1. Genesis 1:1 – God created & rules all things
2. Genesis 1:26-28 – God made man in his image & gave him dominion to rule his creation
3. Genesis 3:6-7 – Man sinned and rejected God's call to rule and represent him in creation
4. Genesis 3:15 – God promised redemption through a descendant of the woman
5. Genesis 12:1-3 – God would bless mankind through Abraham's descendants
6. Genesis 49:10 – God would send a king to bless the world through Judah, a descendant of Abraham
7. Exodus 24:3 – God established a covenant with Israel
8. 2 Samuel 7.12-13 – God would eternally establish the throne of David (a descendant of Judah)
9. Isaiah 53:6 – God promised a servant who would bear man's sins
10. Jeremiah 31:31-34 – God would give a new covenant

The Story of the Bible
In 20 Verses

NEW TESTAMENT (FULFILLMENT)
1. Mark 1:14-15 – Jesus announced that the period of fulfillment had arrived
2. Matthew 16:18 – Jesus promised to build his church, about which his apostles would preach
3. John 19.19-20 – Jesus died for the sins of all mankind
4. Matthew 28:1-10 – Jesus was raised from the dead and seen by many of his disciples
5. Acts 2:17 – On the day of Pentecost, the outpouring of the Spirit meant the Messianic era had come
6. Acts 11:17-18 – The outpouring of the Spirit on the Gentiles meant salvation was for all
7. Romans 3:21-26 – All mankind needs salvation by faith in Christ Jesus
8. Romans 12:1-2 – Salvation in Christ requires a life given to him in sacrifice
9. Romans 16:20 – the victory over Satan was being realized in the NT era
10. Revelation 22:20 – Jesus has promised to return, and his followers eagerly await his arrival

By Way of Reminder
The Beatitudes
See Matthew 5:3-12 (NASB)

VERSE	TRAIT	BLESSING
3	Poor in spirit	Kingdom of heaven
4	Mourn	Shall be comforted
5	Gentle	Shall inherit the earth
6	Hunger & thirst for righteousness	Shall be satisfied
7	Merciful	Shall receive mercy
8	Pure in heart	Shall see God
9	Peacemakers	Shall be called sons of God
10	Persecuted for righteousness' sake	Kingdom of heaven

Model Prayer
See Matthew 6:9-13 (NASB)

Pray, then, in this way:
"Our Father who is in heaven,
    hallowed be Your name.
Your kingdom come.
Your will be done,
    on earth as it is in heaven.
Give us this day our daily bread.
And forgive us our debts,
    as we also have forgiven our debtors.
And do not lead us into temptation,
    but deliver us from evil.
For Yours is the kingdom
    and the power and the glory forever.
Amen."

Bible Lists

Spiritual Gifts
Based upon the NASB

1 Corinthians 12:8-10	1 Corinthians 12:28	Romans 12:6-8	Ephesians 4:11
Word of wisdom	Apostles	Prophecy	Apostles
Word of knowledge	Prophets	Service	Prophets
Faith	Teachers	Teaching	Evangelists
Gifts of healing	Miracles	Exhortation	Pastors
Effecting of miracles	Gifts of healing	Giving	Teachers
Prophecy	Helps	Leading	
Distinguishing of spirits	Administrations	Mercy	
Kinds of tongues	Kinds of tongues		
Interpretation of tongues			

By Way of Reminder

Deeds of the flesh
See Galatians 5:19-21 (NASB)

"Now the deeds of the flesh are evident…"
- Immorality
- Impurity
- Sensuality
- Idolatry
- Sorcery
- Enmities
- Strife
- Jealousy
- Outbursts of anger
- Disputes
- Dissensions
- Factions
- Envying
- Drunkenness
- Carousing
- Things like these

Fruit of the Spirit
See Galatians 5:22-23 (NASB)

"But the fruit of the Spirit is…"
- Love
- Joy
- Peace
- Patience
- Kindness
- Goodness
- Faithfulness
- Gentleness
- Self-control
- Against such things there is no law

Character of Love
See 1 Corinthians 13:4-7 (NASB)

"Love is…"

- Patient
- Kind
- Not jealous
- Does not brag
- Is not arrogant
- Does not act unbecomingly
- Does not seek its own
- Is not provoked
- Does not take into account a wrong suffered
- Does not rejoice in unrighteousness, but rejoices with the truth
- Bears all things
- Believes all things
- Hopes all things
- Endures all things

Armor of God
See Ephesians 6:14-17 (NASB)

Put on the full armor of God…

- Loins girded with truth
- Breastplate of righteousness
- Feet shod with the preparation of the gospel of peace
- Shield of faith
- Helmet of salvation
- Sword of the Spirit

By Way of Reminder

Qualifications of Elders

See 1 Timothy 3:2-7; Titus 1:6-9 (NASB)

1 TIMOTHY 3.2-7

- Above reproach
- Husband of one wife
- Temperate
- Prudent
- Respectable
- Hospitable
- Able to teach
- Not addicted to wine
- Not pugnacious
- Gentle
- Peaceable
- Free from the love of money
- Manages his own household well
- Keeps his children under control with all dignity
- Not a new convert
- Good reputation with those outside the church

Qualifications of Elders (cont.)
See 1 Timothy 3:2-7; Titus 1:6-9 (NASB)

TITUS 1.6-9

- Above reproach
- Husband of one wife
- Having children who believe
- Not accused of dissipation or rebellion
- Above reproach as God's steward
- Not self-willed
- Not quick-tempered
- Not addicted to wine
- Not pugnacious
- Not fond of sordid gain
- Hospitable
- Loving what is good
- Sensible
- Just
- Devout
- Self-controlled
- Holding fast the faithful word
- Able to exhort in sound doctrine
- Able to refute those who contradict

By Way of Reminder
Qualifications of Deacons
See 1 Timothy 3:8-13; Acts 6:3 (NASB)

Deacons must likewise be…
- Men of dignity
- Not double-tongued
- Not addicted to much wine
- Not fond of sordid gain
- Holding to the mystery of the faith with a clear conscience
- First tested
- Beyond reproach

Women [wives] must be…
- Dignified
- Not malicious gossips
- Temperate
- Faithful in all things

Deacons must be…
- Husbands of one wife
- Good managers of their children and their own households

Christian Graces
See 2 Peter 1:5-7 (NASB)

- Faith
- Moral excellence
- Knowledge
- Self-control
- Perseverance
- Godliness
- Brotherly kindness
- Love

By Way of Reminder

Bible Topics & Memory Verses

By Way of Reminder

THE BIBLE
- Deuteronomy 8:3
- Psalm 19:7-11
- Psalm 119:105
- Isaiah 40:8
- 2 Timothy 2:15
- 2 Timothy 3:16-17
- Hebrews 4:12
- 2 Peter 1:20-21

GOD
- Genesis 1:1
- Exodus 34:5-7
- Numbers 23:19
- Deuteronomy 6:4-5
- Deuteronomy 10:17-18
- Psalm 14:1
- Psalm 19:1
- Psalm 90:1-2
- Micah 7:18-19
- John 3:16
- John 4:24
- Romans 11:33-36
- Hebrews 11:6
- 2 Peter 3:9
- 1 John 1:5
- 1 John 4:7-8

JESUS CHRIST
- Matthew 16:15-16
- John 1:1, 14
- John 8:24
- Acts 2:36
- Acts 4:12
- Ephesians 1:22-23
- Philippians 2:5-11
- Colossians 1:15-18
- 1 Timothy 2:5-6

JESUS CHRIST (cont.)
- Hebrews 1:1-2
- Hebrews 13:8
- 1 John 2:1-2
- Revelation 1:5-7

THE HOLY SPIRIT
- Ezekiel 36:26-27
- John 3:5
- John 16:8-11
- John 16:13-14
- Acts 2:38
- Acts 5:32
- Romans 8:9-11
- Romans 8:26-27
- 1 Corinthians 6:19-20
- 1 Corinthians 12:13
- Ephesians 4:30
- Ephesians 5:18-19
- Titus 3:5-6

MAN
- Genesis 1:26-27
- Genesis 9:6
- Psalm 8:3-5
- Psalm 90:10
- Psalm 103:13-16
- Psalm 139:13-14
- Ecclesiastes 7:29
- Acts 17:26-28
- Romans 3:23

SIN
- Genesis 4:7
- Numbers 32:23
- Psalm 32:1-2
- Isaiah 59:1-2
- Ezekiel 18:4
- Romans 3:23

SIN (cont.)
- Romans 5:12
- Romans 6:11-14, 23
- 1 Corinthians 6:9-10
- 1 Corinthians 10:13
- 2 Corinthians 5:21
- James 4:17
- 1 Peter 2:24
- 1 John 1:6-10
- 1 John 3:4

FAITH
- Psalm 37:5
- Psalm 40:4
- Proverbs 3:5-6
- John 3:16
- Romans 3:21-22
- Romans 5:1-2
- Romans 10:17
- 2 Corinthians 5:7
- Galatians 2:20
- Galatians 3:26-27
- Hebrews 11:1, 6
- James 2:14-26
- 1 John 5:4-5

REPENTANCE
- Psalm 32:5-6
- Matthew 3:2
- Acts 2:37-38
- Acts 3.19
- 2 Corinthians 7:9-10
- Hebrews 6:4-6
- 2 Peter 3:9

BAPTISM
- Matthew 28.19
- Mark 16.15-16
- John 3:5

BAPTISM (cont.)
- Acts 2:37-38
- Romans 6:3-4
- 1 Corinthians 12:13
- Galatians 3:26-27
- Titus 3:5
- 1 Peter 3:20-21

SALVATION
- Genesis 49:18
- Exodus 15:2
- 1 Chronicles 16:23
- Psalm 18:2
- Psalm 37:39-40
- Psalm 51:12
- Isaiah 55:6-7
- Acts 4:12
- Romans 1:16-17
- Titus 2:11
- Hebrews 2:9-10
- Hebrews 5:9
- 1 Peter 2:1-2

FORGIVENESS
- Proverbs 17:9
- Matthew 6:14-15
- Ephesians 1:7
- Ephesians 4:32
- Colossians 3:12-13
- 1 John 1:8-9

THE CHURCH
- Isaiah 2.2-3
- Matthew 16.18
- 1 Corinthians 3.11
- 1 Corinthians 12.12-13
- Ephesians 1.22-23
- Ephesians 2.19-22

By Way of Reminder

THE CHURCH (cont.)
- Ephesians 3:10-11
- 1 Timothy 3:15
- Hebrews 12:22-24

GROWTH
- Ephesians 4:15
- Philippians 1:9-11
- Colossians 1:9-12
- 1 Peter 2:1-3
- 2 Peter 1:5-8
- 2 Peter 3:18

ANGER
- Proverbs 14:29
- Proverbs 15:1, 18
- Proverbs 16:32
- Proverbs 29:11
- Proverbs 30:33
- Ecclesiastes 7:9
- Romans 12:17-19
- Ephesians 4:26-27
- Colossians 3:8
- James 1:19-20

ASSURANCE
- Job 19.25-26
- Psalm 23.4
- Psalm 46.1-3
- Psalm 73.25-26
- Psalm 118.5-6
- Romans 8.28-39
- Hebrews 4.16
- 1 Peter 1.3-5
- 2 Peter 1.10-11

CHILDREN
- (See "Family")

COMFORT
- (See "Grief")

DOUBT
- (See "Faith")

DEATH
- Genesis 2:16-17
- Genesis 3:19
- Psalm 23:4
- Psalm 39:4-5
- Psalm 90:9-10, 12
- Psalm 116:15
- Ecclesiastes 7:1-2
- Romans 5:12
- Romans 6:23
- Romans 8:37-39
- 1 Corinthians 15:54-57
- Philippians 1:21
- Hebrews 2:14-15
- Hebrews 9:27-28
- Revelation 14:13

DEPRESSION
- (See "Discouragement")

DISCOURAGEMENT
- Genesis 4.6-7
- Psalm 34.8-9, 15-18
- Psalm 42.5
- Proverbs 13.12
- Proverbs 17.22
- Isaiah 12.1-2
- Romans 15.13
- 2 Corinthians 4.7-10, 16-18
- Philippians 4.4-9, 12-13
- Hebrews 12.12-13

ENCOURAGEMENT
- Joshua 1:9
- Psalm 27:10
- Psalm 34:4
- Psalm 42:11
- Psalm 71:17-18
- Psalm 94:19
- Psalm 103:1-5
- Psalm 147:1-3
- Proverbs 18:24
- Isaiah 43:1-2
- Matthew 11:27-30
- John 11:25-26
- John 14:1-4
- Romans 5:1-5
- Romans 8:18
- 1 Corinthians 15:58
- 2 Corinthians 4:7-10
- 2 Corinthians 12:9
- Philippians 4:4-6
- 1 Peter 5:6-7, 10
- Revelation 21:3-4

ENVY
- Psalm 37:1
- Proverbs 23:17
- Proverbs 24:1, 19
- Romans 1:28-32
- Galatians 5:19-21
- Titus 3:3
- James 3:13-18
- 1 Peter 2:1-3

FAMILY
- Genesis 2:18, 24
- Genesis 18:19
- Exodus 20:12

FAMILY (cont.)
- Deuteronomy 6:6-7
- Joshua 24:15
- Psalm 103:17-18
- Psalm 127
- Psalm 128
- Proverbs 13:22
- Proverbs 15:20
- Proverbs 17:6
- Proverbs 20:7
- Proverbs 22:6
- Ephesians 6:1-4
- Colossians 3:20-21
- 1 Timothy 5:8
- 3 John 4

FATHERS
- (See "Men")

FEAR
- Deuteronomy 31:6
- Joshua 1:9
- Psalm 27:1
- Psalm 34:4
- Psalm 118:6
- Proverbs 29:25
- Matthew 10:28
- John 14:27
- 2 Timothy 1:7
- Hebrews 2:14-15
- 1 Peter 3:6, 13-14
- 1 John 4:17-18

FRIENDSHIP
- Proverbs 13:20
- Proverbs 17:17
- Proverbs 19:6
- Proverbs 22:24-25
- Proverbs 23:20-21

FRIENDSHIP (cont.)
- Proverbs 27:6, 10
- John 15:12-15
- 1 Corinthians 15:33
- 2 Corinthians 6:14-18

GOSSIP
- Proverbs 10:18
- Proverbs 11:13
- Proverbs 18:8
- Proverbs 20:19
- Proverbs 26:20-21
- James 4:11

GRATITUDE
- Psalm 95:2
- Psalm 107:1
- Colossians 2:7
- Philippians 4:4-7
- 1 Thessalonians 5:16-18
- 1 Timothy 4:4-5
- Hebrews 12:28-29
- Hebrews 13:15

GRIEF
- Psalm 23:4
- Psalm 34:18
- Psalm 46:1
- Psalm 116:15
- Proverbs 14:13
- Proverbs 15:13
- Matthew 5:4
- John 11:35
- John 16:20-22
- Romans 8:38-39
- 2 Corinthians 1:3-4
- 1 Thessalonians 4:13-18
- Revelation 21:3-4

GUILT
- Psalm 32
- Psalm 38:3-4
- Psalm 40:12
- Luke 18:13-14
- Romans 3:23-25a
- 1 John 1:8-1

HAPPINESS
- (See "Joy")

HEALTH
- Psalm 23
- Mark 1:29-34
- Mark 6:53-56
- 2 Corinthians 4:16 - 5.6
- 2 Corinthians 12:1-10

HOMOSEXUALITY
- Leviticus 18:22, 24
- Leviticus 20:13
- Judges 19:22-23
- Romans 1:26-27
- 1 Corinthians 6:9-10
- 1 Timothy 1:8-11

HOPE
- Psalm 33:18
- Psalm 42:5
- Proverbs 10:28
- Proverbs 13:12
- Romans 8:24-25
- Romans 15:4
- Ephesians 1:18-19
- 1 Thessalonians 4:13-18
- Hebrews 6:17-20
- 1 Peter 3:15
- 1 John 3:3

HUMILITY
- Psalm 25:9
- Psalm 138:6
- Psalm 147:6
- Proverbs 15:33
- Proverbs 16:19
- Proverbs 22:4
- Proverbs 29:23
- Matthew 5:3, 5
- Matthew 18:1-4
- Galatians 6:1-2
- Philippians 2:3-4, 5-11
- Colossians 3:12-13
- James 4:6, 10
- 1 Peter 5:5-7

HUSBANDS
- (See "Men")

JOY
- Nehemiah 8:10
- Psalm 2:11
- Psalm 5:11
- Psalm 9:1-2
- Psalm 30:4-5
- Ecclesiastes 2:24-26
- Ecclesiastes 3:12-14
- Isaiah 12:2-3
- Romans 15:13
- Galatians 5:22-23
- Philippians 4:4-7
- James 5:13
- 1 Peter 1:8-9

LAZINESS
- Proverbs 6.6-11
- Proverbs 10.4-5, 26
- Proverbs 13.4

LAZINESS (cont.)
- Proverbs 15:19
- Proverbs 18:9
- Proverbs 19:15, 24
- Proverbs 20:4
- Proverbs 22:13
- Proverbs 24:30-34
- Proverbs 26:13-16
- Ecclesiastes 10:18
- Matthew 25:26
- 2 Thessalonians 3:6-12

LONELINESS
- Deuteronomy 31:6
- Joshua 1:5, 9
- 1 Kings 19:10
- Psalm 25:16
- Psalm 27:7-10
- Psalm 68:6
- Isaiah 41:10
- Matthew 11:27-30
- 2 Timothy 4:16-18

LOVE FOR GOD
- Deuteronomy 6:5
- Psalm 37:4
- Psalm 145:20
- Matthew 22:34-40
- John 14:15
- Romans 8:28-30
- 1 John 5:3

LOVE FOR OTHERS
- Leviticus 19:18
- Proverbs 10:12
- Proverbs 17:9, 17
- Matthew 5:43-47
- Matthew 22:37-40
- John 13:34-35

By Way of Reminder

LOVE FOR OTHERS (cont.)
- 1 Corinthians 13:4-7
- Galatians 5:22-23
- Hebrews 10:24-25
- 1 Peter 1:22-23
- 1 John 3:16-18
- 1 John 4:7-11, 20-21

LUST
- Exodus 20:14, 17
- Job 31:1, 9-12
- Matthew 5:27-30
- Romans 1:24
- Romans 6:12-14
- Romans 13:13-14
- 1 Corinthians 9:24-27
- 2 Timothy 2:22
- James 1:13-15
- 1 Peter 1:14-16
- 1 Peter 2:11
- 1 Peter 4:1-3
- 2 Peter 1:4
- 1 John 2:15-17

LYING
- Exodus 20:16
- Proverbs 12:19, 22
- Ephesians 4:25
- Colossians 3:9
- Revelation 21:8

MARRIAGE
- Genesis 2:20-25
- Proverbs 18:22
- Proverbs 21:9, 19
- Matthew 19:3-9
- 1 Corinthians 7:1-5, 9

MARRIAGE (cont.)
- Ephesians 5:22-33
- Colossians 3:18-19
- Hebrews 13:4
- 1 Peter 3:1-7

MEN
- Psalm 119:9
- Proverbs 27:17
- 1 Corinthians 11:2-16
- Ephesians 5:22-33
- Ephesians 6:4
- Colossians 3:19, 21
- 1 Timothy 5:8
- Titus 2:2, 6-8

MONEY
- (See "Wealth")

MOTHERS
- (See "Women")

OBEDIENCE
- 1 Samuel 15:22-23
- Proverbs 19:16
- Luke 17:9-10
- John 14:15
- John 15:14
- Acts 4:19-20
- Acts 5:29
- Ephesians 6:1
- Hebrews 5:8-10
- Hebrews 13:17
- 1 Peter 1:22-23

PARENTS
- (See "Family")

PATIENCE
- Psalm 37:7-9
- Psalm 40:1
- Romans 5:3-5
- Galatians 5:22-23
- 1 Thessalonians 5:14
- James 1:2-4

PEACE
- Proverbs 16:7
- Proverbs 17:1
- Matthew 5:9
- John 14:27
- Romans 5:1
- Romans 12:18
- Romans 14:19
- Galatians 5:22-23
- Ephesians 2:14-18
- Philippians 4:4-9
- Colossians 3:15
- Hebrews 12:14

PERSECUTION
- Matthew 5:10-12
- Matthew 5:44-45
- Acts 14:22
- Romans 8:35-39
- Philippians 1:27-30
- 2 Timothy 3:12
- 1 Peter 4:16
- Revelation 2:10

PERSEVERANCE
- Romans 5:3-5
- Romans 15:4
- 1 Timothy 6:11
- 2 Timothy 2:11-13
- Hebrews 12:1-2

PERSEVERANCE (cont.)
- James 1:2-4, 12
- James 5:11
- Revelation 2.10

PORNOGRAPHY
- (See "Lust")

PRAISE
- Psalm 8:1-2
- Psalm 100:1-5
- Psalm 147:1
- Psalm 148:1-14
- Psalm 150:1-6
- Romans 11:33-36
- Romans 16:25-27
- Ephesians 3:20-21
- 1 Timothy 1:17
- Jude 24-25

PRAYER
- Psalm 34:15
- Psalm 65:1-2
- Psalm 145:18-19
- Proverbs 15:8
- Proverbs 28:9
- Jeremiah 29:4-7
- Matthew 5:44-45a
- Matthew 6:5-6
- Romans 8:26-27
- Philippians 4:4-7
- 1 Thessalonians 5:16-18
- Hebrews 4:16
- James 1:5-8
- James 5:13-18
- 1 John 5:13-15

By Way of Reminder

PRIDE
- Proverbs 8:13
- Proverbs 16:18
- Proverbs 29:23
- Luke 9:23
- Philippians 2:3-4
- 1 Peter 5:5

SEX AND LUST
- Genesis 2:24-25
- Matthew 5:27-28
- 1 Corinthians 6:19-20
- Colossians 3:5
- 1 Thessalonians 4:3-5
- 2 Timothy 2:22
- 1 Peter 2:11
- 1 John 2:15-17

SICKNESS
- (See "Health")

TEMPTATION
- Genesis 4:6-7
- Psalm 119:11
- Matthew 26:41
- 1 Corinthians 10:13
- Galatians 6:1
- 1 Timothy 6:9-10
- James 1:13-15
- 1 John 2:15-17

THANKFULNESS
- (See "Gratitude")

WEALTH
- Deuteronomy 8:11-18
- Proverbs 10:4
- Proverbs 22:2

WEALTH (cont.)
- Proverbs 23:4-5
- Matthew 19:23-26
- Luke 12.15
- 1 Timothy 6.9-10, 17-19

WIVES
- (See "Women")

WOMEN
- Genesis 1:26-27
- Genesis 2:22-25
- Proverbs 11:22
- Proverbs 21:9, 19
- Proverbs 31:10, 30
- 1 Corinthians 11:2-16
- 1 Corinthians 14:34-35
- Galatians 3:28
- Ephesians 5:22-33
- 1 Timothy 2:9-15
- 1 Timothy 5:1-2
- Titus 2:3-5

WORK
- Proverbs 10:4
- Proverbs 18:9
- Ecclesiastes 9:10
- John 6:27
- Colossians 3:23-24
- 2 Thessalonians 3:8
- 1 Timothy 5:8

WORRY
- Psalm 139:23
- Isaiah 35:4
- Matthew 6:25, 34
- Philippians 4:6
- 1 Peter 5:6-7

WORSHIP
- Psalm 29:1-2
- Psalm 66:1-4
- Psalm 95:1-6
- Matthew 15:7-9
- John 4:20-24
- Acts 17:22-31
- Romans 12:1-2
- Hebrews 12:22-24
- 1 Peter 2:4-5

YOUTH
- Psalm 71:5
- Psalm 119:9
- Proverbs 20:29
- Ecclesiastes 11:9–12:1
- 1 Timothy 4:12

ZEAL
- Psalm 69:9
- Romans 10:2
- Titus 2:14
- 1 Peter 3:13

www.ingramcontent.com/pod-product-compliance
Lightning Source LLC
Chambersburg PA
CBHW070451050426
42451CB00015B/3440